Zac Newton Investigates

Spectacular Space

WORLD BOOK

www.worldbook.com

World Book, Inc.
180 North LaSalle Street
Suite 900
Chicago, Illinois 60601
USA

For information about other World Book publications,
visit our website at www.worldbook.com or call
1-800-WORLDBK (967-5325).

For information about sales to schools and libraries,
call 1-800-975-3250 (United States), or 1-800-837-5365
(Canada).

Library of Congress Cataloging-in-Publication Data for
this volume has been applied for.

This edition: ISBN: 978-0-7166-4061-5 (hc.)
ISBN: 978-0-7166-4056-1 (set, hc.)

Also available as: ISBN: 978-0-7166-4067-7 (e-book)

Printed in China by Shenzhen Wing King Tong Paper
Products Co., Ltd., Shenzhen, Guangdong
1st printing July 2018

Produced for World Book by
White-Thomson Publishing Ltd

www.wtpub.co.uk

Author: Paul Harrison

Editor: Izzi Howell

Design/Art director: Claire Gaukrodger

Illustrator: Rob Davis/The Art Agency

Cover artwork: © Doug Holgate

Staff

A glossary of terms appears on p. 94.

Contents

Zac Newton and friends

Zac

Zac is a junior genius and inventor of the Backspace app. The app allows Zac and his friends to take virtual trips through time and space, just by snapping a selfie.

Lucía

Lucía has a sharp mind and an even sharper wit. She pretends to be too cool for school, but inside she burns to learn about science.

Marcus

Quick-thinking Marcus is always ready with a joke. Although he loves to clown around, he knows more than he lets on.

Ning

Ning likes to run, jump, and play ball. She may be the youngest of the group, but nobody's going to push her around.

Orbit

Zac's dog, Orbit, loves to join Zac and his friends on their adventures. He's not afraid of anything—except loud noises.

Chapter 1

Cloud Cover

It was all set to be a perfect night for stargazing. Zac Newton had set up his brand-new telescope in the front yard. He had his star charts unfolded and some snacks ready for the long evening ahead. His best friends—Lucía, Marcus, and Ning—had come over, too. Zac had spent the day telling them about all the amazing things that they were going to see. There was just one problem—the sky was completely clouded over.

"Sorry, friends, the weather forecast said it was supposed to be clear tonight," said Zac.

"Don't worry about it, Zac," said Lucía. "We'll do something else. It's been a while since we had a chance just to hang out together. Besides, I wasn't excited about standing in the dark all night anyway."

"And we still have the snacks!" said Ning.

"Now you're talking!" said Lucía.

"You want some, Marcus?" asked Ning.

"No, I'm fine, thanks," said Marcus.

"What?" cried Ning. "Usually, you're a total snack monster!"

"Are you sure you're okay? You look kind of sad," said Lucía.

"Yeah, you haven't even teased me about my star party being ruined," Zac added.

"I know I've said before that I wish you were quieter,"

joked Ning, "but now that my wish has come true, it's kind of freaky."

"Sorry, friends, I have some bad news," said Marcus. "Well, it's good news, I guess. My mom has been offered a promotion at work."

"Hey, that is good news," said Lucía.

"So, what's the problem?" asked Zac.

"The job's not here. We'd have to move," Marcus replied.

"Move? Where to?" asked Ning.

"Alaska," said Marcus softly.

"ALASKA!" the friends cried together.

"I know!" answered Marcus. "Mom says it's a cool place—well, really, a cold place—but I'll be so far away from you all! There's even Canada between here and there, and Canada is one huge country!"

Ning thought for a moment. "Don't they have

beautiful mountains in Alaska?"

"Right, Ning," said Zac. "Marcus, you could visit Denali, the tallest mountain in the United States!"

"When are you leaving?" asked Lucía.

"I don't know yet," Marcus said. "Maybe in a month or so? My parents are trying to work out the details."

"How long does it take to get there?" asked Ning.

"Like, forever," Marcus answered. "You can probably get to the moon faster."

"Alaska is way better than the moon," said Zac. He pulled up an article on Alaska on his cell phone and began listing attractions. "You could hike Mendenhall Glacier... watch moose in Chugach National Forest..."

"All while getting frostbite," whined Marcus.

"You just have to dress warm," said Zac. "You'd be way happier in Alaska than on the moon."

"Could a person even live on the moon?" asked Ning.

"There's not much on the moon," Zac replied. "And believe me, you wouldn't want to live there."

"I'd at least like to give it a try," said Marcus.

"Really? The moon? Not for me, thanks," said Lucía. "All the fun stuff is down here on Earth."

"Look, there's an easy way to settle this," said Zac.

"The Backspace app?" said Ning.

"You bet," said Zac, pulling his cell phone from the pocket of his jacket. "The Backspace app is my greatest invention. It can take us on a virtual visit to any time and place. All we have to do is gather for a selfie..."

Zac hugged his friends in close. Then, holding the phone at arm's length, he framed them all in the screen and hit the Backspace button.

FLASH!

ZUMMMMMMmmmmmmmm...

The scene around them changed instantly. A moment ago, they had been hanging out in Zac's front yard. Now, they appeared to be standing on the moon. The trees and houses of Zac's neighborhood had been replaced by craters, rocks, and broad plains covered in powdery dust.

"Whoa, this is weird," said Ning. "It's bright daylight, but the sky is black."

"That's because there's no real atmosphere here," said Zac. "On Earth, the sky looks blue because of the air. When sunlight strikes the air, the air scatters it, bouncing light off in different directions. More blue light is scattered to the surface than any other color. That's what makes the sky look blue. Here on the moon, there is no air. So there's no blue sky, either."

"No air! So how can we breathe?" gasped Marcus.

"This is all virtual reality, remember? We're still in my front yard, not actually on the moon," Zac explained.

"Is that … Earth?" said Lucía, pointing upward.

A bright blue and green ball glowed against the darkness of space.

"Yes, that's Earth," said Zac. "Beautiful, isn't it?"

"Amazing," said Ning.

"There's most of the United States," said Ning, pointing to the center of North America. "And that's Alaska over there."

"From up here, Alaska doesn't look that far from home," said Ning.

Lucía stood frowning at the moon's surface. "Why are there so many holes in the ground?" she asked.

"They're not holes, they're craters. The moon has been hit by rocks from space for millions of years, and these are the marks they have left behind," said Zac.

"So why does the moon get hit by so many space rocks but Earth doesn't?" asked Marcus.

"That's because of our atmosphere, too," said Zac. "Rocks fall toward Earth, too. But as rocks fall through Earth's atmosphere, they rub against the air, producing friction. The friction heats them up. Most burn up completely before they reach Earth's surface."

"Wow, so the atmosphere isn't just pretty, it also protects us," said Marcus.

"Look at the ground," said Ning, pointing down. "Except for the craters, it looks like fresh snowfall or a deserted beach. There's not even a footprint."

"That's all about to change," said Zac. "Look behind you."

Where Zac's house had been, there stood a spaceship. It was not big and sleek like the spaceships they had seen in movies. Its top half looked like a jumble of metal boxes. The bottom half was covered in foil that shimmered gold in the sunlight. A ladder stretched from its top to the ground below.

"That ship is the Eagle lander," Zac explained. "It's from the Apollo 11 mission."

"Oh, oh, I know about this," said Marcus. "That was when people landed on the moon for the first time! There were two astronauts, Neil Armstrong and Buzz … Lightyear? No, that's not right."

"Buzz Aldrin," laughed Zac. "And, you're right. It was the first time people walked on the moon. There were actually three astronauts on the mission. Michael Collins stayed in the command module, another part of the Apollo craft. Collins circled the moon in the command module, while the other two astronauts came down in the lander."

"That lander's not very big," said Lucía. "I wouldn't want to be cooped up in there!"

"Look!" said Zac.

An astronaut was walking slowly across the surface of the moon.

"Let's watch from behind this rock," said Zac. "We don't want to freak anybody out. Come here, Orbit."

"That's Neil Armstrong," said Zac. "He's the first person to set foot on the moon."

"I always wondered," said Marcus, "why do they wear those big, clumsy space suits?"

"To keep them alive," Zac explained. "They need air to breathe, because there's no atmosphere. The suit provides that. It also keeps the astronauts warm, because it's freezing cold on the moon. And, it protects them against harmful rays from the sun. We don't need to wear spacesuits on Earth…"

"Because of the atmosphere?" guessed Ning.

"You know it!" Zac smiled.

"All the more reason to stay on Earth," said Lucía.

"Look at the way he's walking!" said Ning. They watched Armstrong bounce slowly from one foot to another, taking huge strides. "I'd love to be that bouncy! Think of the high jump records I could break!"

"He moves like that because the pull of gravity here is much weaker than on Earth's surface. Gravity is the force that pulls us toward the ground. A weaker pull of gravity makes it easier to bounce and float."

"Yeah, that's pretty cool," said Marcus. "I could handle that."

"If you like bouncing, Marcus, get a trampoline," said Ning. "Then even I might come to Alaska for a visit."

Chapter 2

Rocks and Hard Places

Zac tapped the screen of his cell phone, and he and his friends were back in his front yard.

"It always takes my brain a second to adjust when that happens," said Lucía.

"Did you mean what you said, Ning—that you would come and visit me in Alaska?" Marcus asked.

"Yeah, of course I would," Ning replied. "I need you around to make me look good." She gave him a playful poke on the arm.

"I'll come, too," said Zac. "We all will, won't we Lucía?"

"Sure," said Lucía, "it's only an airplane ride."

"Will you really?" said Marcus. "It's a long way to Alaska, isn't it?"

"Well, yes and no," said Zac. "It's a long way, but not compared with space travel."

"Oh, space, space, space," muttered Lucía.

"What do you have against space?" asked Zac.

"Well, what's so great about it?" Lucía huffed. "We've been to the moon, and that was just dust and holes. I like things here on Earth, with trees and grass and animals and weather."

"But space is amazing and beautiful and, and…" Zac stammered. "I know—we should take a tour of the solar system."

"The what, now?" said Marcus.

"The solar system—that's what we call all the planets and other things that orbit our particular star, the sun," Zac explained.

"The sun's a star?" said Ning.

"It is, but I'll get to that later," said Zac. He tapped the screen of his phone, and it projected a three-dimensional image of the solar system. The sun

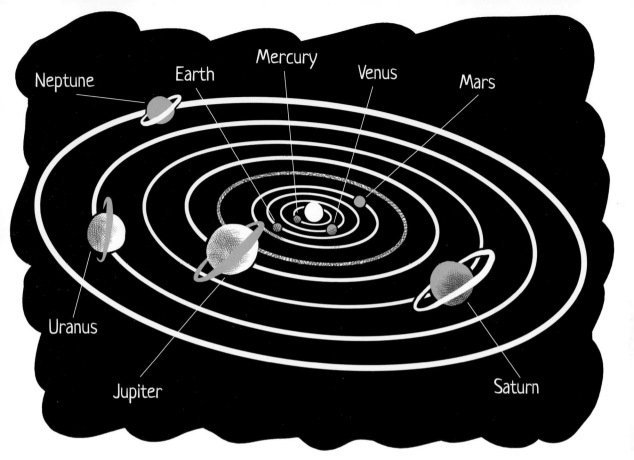

hovered in the air before them, with Earth and the other planets circling around it.

"See, this is what the solar system looks like, "said Zac. "We'll take a flying tour. I guarantee it will change your mind."

"Whatever," said Lucía doubtfully.

"Hey, even Orbit's coming," said Zac. The dog wandered over and gave them a curious look.

"Good, gather around, everyone," said Zac.

FLASH!

ZUMMMMMMmmmmmmmm...

A new virtual world surrounded the friends. The ground at their feet was covered in silvery dust and dotted with craters.

"Are we back on the moon again?" said Ning.

"It looks like it, doesn't it? But no, this is the planet Mercury," said Zac.

"Look how big and bright the sun looks!" said Marcus, shielding his eyes.

"Yeah, Mercury is the planet closest to the sun," said Zac. "Now, Mercury here is actually made up of pretty much the same stuff as Earth."

"You're joking," said Marcus. "And, that's my job."

"Mercury is one of the four planets called *rocky* planets," Zac explained. "That's because they're made up of basically, well, rock."

"Is Mercury the same size as Earth?" asked Ning.

"No, it's much smaller." Zac reached into his pocket and pulled out a baseball, cupping it in his palm. "If Earth were the size of this baseball, then Mercury would only be about the size of a golf ball."

"A smaller planet means a weaker gravitational pull," Zac continued. "So, you'll feel lighter here than you do on Earth—kind of like on the moon," said Zac.

"Yeah, I can see that," called Ning, bounding around them in big, bouncing strides.

"If Mercury is like Earth, where are all the plants and animals and stuff?" asked Marcus.

"Mercury is too close to the sun, and its gravitational pull is too weak," Zac explained. "Any atmosphere it may have had was blown away by the sun's energy long ago. So, there's nothing to breathe and nothing to protect the surface against the intense sunlight. In short, Mercury's not a great place to live."

"I kind of like it," said Ning, bounding around.

"Come on, we can't spend our entire tour at the first stop. Let's go check out Earth's twin planet," said Zac.

"I hope it's more exciting than this one," said Lucía.

FLASH!

ZUMMMMMMmmmmmmmm...

The scene around them changed again. The friends were standing on a cracked and broken plain. Huge peaks rose in the distance. It was a hot and dry place.

"I guess you didn't mean Earth's *identical* twin," said Marcus.

"You're right," said Zac. "Venus is called Earth's twin because it's just about the same size as Earth. But

Venus is much closer to the sun. It takes Earth 365 days to travel around the sun. Venus's much smaller orbit takes only about 225 days."

"Is there any water here?" asked Ning, kicking at the dry ground.

"Not on the surface," answered Zac. "And, there are only traces of water in the atmosphere."

"At least this planet has clouds," said Lucía, pointing up.

"Yes, but they're made of sulfuric acid," said Zac.

"Is everything here terrible?" asked Lucía.

"Pretty much," Zac said. "You couldn't breathe here. The air is mainly made up of a gas called carbon dioxide, and there's very little oxygen. Also—though we don't feel it, because we aren't actually here, I mean, there—the surface temperature is around 870 °F. That's 465 °C, way hotter than an oven."

"On the real Venus, we'd be burned to a crisp!" said Lucía.

"What are those?" said Marcus, pointing toward some distant mountains. "They look like volcanoes."

"Exactly," said Zac. "You know, ancient people named Venus for the Roman goddess of love. They might have picked a different name if they'd seen it up close."

"Venus has volcanoes—okay, that's a bit more interesting, but you'll have to do better than that to impress me," said Lucía.

"Well, I wouldn't want to live here," said Marcus. "Alaska is looking better all the time."

"Can we get going?" asked Ning.

"Yes, I think it's time to visit Earth's other neighbor," said Zac, tapping his phone again.

FLASH!

ZUMMMMMMmmmmmmmm...

"Welcome to Mars—the red planet," said Zac, holding his arms out wide. "I'll admit that it doesn't look like much, but it's a lot more like Earth than it appears."

"So, why is the ground all red?" asked Ning.

"That's the iron in the rocks and dust," said Zac.

"Great, a rusty planet," said Lucía. "If I wanted to see rust, I'd just hang out in a junkyard."

"Tornado!" shouted Marcus.

In the distance, a large column of dust was twirling its way across the landscape.

"It's a dust devil," said Zac, "a tiny storm that looks like a tornado. Mars has bigger dust storms, too. The biggest ones can pretty much cover the planet. And, if there are dust storms, there has to be wind. This is one of the things that makes Mars like Earth."

"Is there anything else?" asked Marcus.

"Well, it has clouds, and more important, frozen water," Zac replied.

"You mean ice? Why's that important?" asked Ning.

"Well," said Zac, "scientists have dreamed of building settlements on Mars where people can live. Human explorers could come here to learn more about the planet and space in general. We could even use Mars as a base of operations, launching rockets from here to explore farther out into the solar system."

"And Mars's water makes that possible?" asked Marcus.

"Well, it's one of the things. Water is incredibly heavy to carry around, so if you have a source of water close by, it's really handy. The gravitational pull of Mars is also lower than that of Earth, making it easier to launch rockets."

"I have to admit, living on another planet is starting to sound pretty cool," said Ning.

"I think I'd rather live in Alaska with Marcus," said Lucía.

"How long would it take to get here, Zac?" asked Marcus.

"About six months," Zac answered.

"Wow, that's a long trip," said Marcus. "You could practically walk to Alaska in that time!"

Chapter 3

Gods and Giants

Zac tapped the button on his app, and the friends found themselves back in his yard. Zac pushed the phone back into his pocket. "I'd better get this telescope put away," he said.

"Hold on a minute," said Marcus. "If the planets we've visited so far aren't right for us to live on, what about the other ones? There are other planets in the solar system, aren't there?"

"Yes, there are four more," Zac replied.

"Come on, then, let's see them," said Marcus.

"Oh, great, more dusty rocks," said Lucía.

"No, not these planets," said Zac. Orbit gave Zac a quick look. "Are you coming, boy?" Zac asked. Orbit turned and padded back to the house.

"Looks like Orbit isn't convinced that these will be any better," said Lucía. "Maybe I'll stay with him."

"Trust me, you won't want to miss this," said Zac.

"Have I ever let any of you down?"

"How about that time you designed a racing cart for me to drive in the big race?" said Ning. "Remember— the racing cart you forgot to make brakes for?"

"Ah, yes… but you did win the race," said Zac.

"I crashed into a duck pond!" Ning cried.

"Look, just trust me," said Zac. Before anyone could argue further, he opened up the Backspace app.

FLASH!

ZUMMMMMMmmmmmmm...

When the new scene had formed around them, the friends were soaring through virtual space.

"Now THIS is more like it!" shouted Ning.

Ahead of them was a giant planet streaked with swirling belts of white and orange stripes.

"That's Jupiter, the biggest planet in our solar system," said Zac. "It has more mass—more

material—than all the other planets in the solar system put together. Those bands of color you see are actually clouds in Jupiter's atmosphere. Scientists call the bright bands *zones* and the dark ones *belts*."

"What's that big red oval?" asked Lucía.

"That's a storm," said Zac. "That one spot is wider across than Earth! Scientists think the storm might have started over 300 years ago."

"Okay, I admit it—that's impressive," said Lucía.

"I hope we're not landing near that," said Ning.

"We can't land on Jupiter—or any of the next few planets—because they're all made of gas. That's why people call them gas giants," Zac explained.

"If it's gas, can't we just fly right through it?" asked Ning with an excited smile.

"Unfortunately, no," smiled Zac. "The weight of all that gas presses down, putting pressure on Jupiter, just like atmospheric pressure on Earth. As you drop through Jupiter's atmosphere, the pressure gets greater and the atmosphere gets thicker until, far below those clouds, the gas turns into a liquid..."

"I don't mind getting wet," said Ning.

"Even if you could survive the pressure," said Zac, "Jupiter might have a core of rock. You don't want to go splatting into that—even if it's just a virtual splat."

The friends streaked past the gigantic planet, admiring its huge size.

"What's that circling around it?" asked Marcus.

"Those are rings of dust," Zac explained. "There are four of them. They're pretty faint, but I'm going to show you a planet with some real rings, now."

The children sped up, zipping through the darkness of space. In no time, they reached their next destination.

"Here we are," said Zac, "the second biggest planet in our solar system and another gas giant—Saturn."

They zoomed over the bright, wide rings circling the planet. "Oh, they're beautiful," Lucía, gasped.

"I didn't know that they stretch so far," said Ning, "or that there are so many of them."

"Let's get a closer look," said Zac plunging towards the rings. "There are actually four main rings, and many fainter ones."

"Are they made of the same stuff as Jupiter's rings?" asked Marcus.

"Not quite. Jupiter's rings are made of dust. These rings are mainly made of ice. There's a lot more mass in these rings, too. Some of the chunks are actually as big as mountains."

The friends flew through one of the rings, dodging the icy boulders.

"The rings aren't very deep," said Ning, as they came out the other side.

"You're right!" said Zac. "For the most part, they're less than about 100 feet or 30 meters deep, but they're wide—nearly 180,000 miles or 290,000 kilometers across!"

"I could fly around these forever," said Ning.

"No time," said Zac. "We have two more planets to see."

Soon the friends arrived at the next planet, a giant, pale blue globe.

"This is Uranus," said Zac. "This is the farthest planet from the sun that you can see without using a telescope. It's roughly 1,800,000,000 miles or

2,900,000,000 kilometers from the sun."

"That's a long way away!" gasped Lucía.

"And, because it's so far from the sun, it's really cold—about −320 °F, or almost −200 °C, where the surface would be. Being a gas giant, like Jupiter and Saturn, it doesn't really have a solid surface."

"Compared to Saturn, it looks a little boring," sniffed Marcus.

"There is something amazing about Uranus, though," said Zac. "Uranus spins on its side, almost as if it's been knocked over. If you think of Earth as spinning like a globe, Uranus spins on its side, like a bicycle wheel."

"Now, follow me!" said Zac, racing off.

Moments later, they were circling a planet again.

"How did we end up back at Uranus?" asked Lucía.

"It looks like Uranus, doesn't it?" Zac replied. "But this is Neptune. Earth's not the only planet that has a twin. Uranus and Neptune are almost the same size, and they're made of the same things. Neptune doesn't lean on its side, though."

"These planets have weird names," said Ning.

"Well, they wouldn't sound so weird if you were an ancient Roman," said Zac. He grabbed his phone. "I know someone we can ask about it. We'll need to use the translate function, too. We're going back to 1782, to what is now Germany, to talk to Johann Bode," he announced, pronouncing it *YOH hahn BOW duh.*

FLASH!

ZUMMMMMMmmmmmmmm...

A man stood next to a desk covered in star charts and drawings of the solar system. He wore a heavy coat with a high collar and a tie that looked like a scarf, tied tight around his neck. The man glanced up from his work and motioned the friends over.

"There it is," he said pointing to a chart. "The newest planet, which I propose to call Uranus."

"Newest?" whispered Marcus.

"Yes, Uranus has only just been discovered. People don't even know about Neptune yet," Zac whispered.

"Why Uranus?" asked Lucía.

"Two reasons," Bode explained. "First, the known planets are named after the Roman gods, so it is perfectly logical to name the new planet following this tradition."

"That makes sense," Lucía admitted.

"Second, this planet follows Saturn in order. Saturn follows Jupiter. In mythology, Saturn is the father of Jupiter. So, to be logical, we should name the new planet after Saturn's father, Uranus."

Marcus burst out laughing. "If they'd named it after my dad, then there'd be a planet called Brandon," he said.

Bode and the children all laughed.

Chapter 4
Dwarfs and Omens

With a tap of Zac's phone, the astronomer disappeared. However, instead of returning to Zac's front yard, the friends found themselves back in space.

"Why are we still out here?" asked Lucía.

"Since we've come all this way, I thought we should see what lies beyond the eight planets," Zac answered. "And, I have a question for you: When is a planet not a planet?"

"What are you talking about?" said Marcus.

"Follow me and find out," said Zac.

The friends zipped through virtual space. They soon arrived at a dark, icy ball.

"And the answer is," said Zac, "when it's Pluto!"

"What do you mean Pluto isn't a planet?" asked Ning.

"Well, Pluto is made of rock and ice, so it's more solid than the gas giants," Zac explained. "However, Pluto is tiny—only one fifth as wide across as Earth."

"That's smaller than the moon," said Lucía.

"Yes, and that turned out to be a problem for Pluto," Zac explained. "When Pluto was discovered, in 1930, people thought it was yet another planet. But in the early 2000's, astronomers started discovering all kinds of similar objects way out here. Many of them are around the same size as Pluto, and they all sort of occupy the same region of the solar system. It seemed confusing to consider them all planets."

"In 2006, astronomers voted to call all these objects 'dwarf planets.' They're round, like planets. But they're not quite big enough to clear everything out of their orbits, the way Earth and the other planets do. Pluto became a dwarf planet. Before that, there were nine planets in our solar system. Now we only have eight."

"They threw Pluto out of the planet club because it was too small?" said Ning.

"Hey, Ning, you're pretty small," Marcus joked. "What if we threw you out?"

"Don't even try it, Mr. Alaska! Actually, look. The surface of Pluto is covered in ice. Maybe you should move here instead," teased Ning.

"Pluto is even colder than Alaska," Zac said. "In fact, it's one of the coldest places in the solar system because it's so far from the sun. It's about 40 times farther from the sun than Earth. Pluto takes 248 Earth *years* to travel around the sun."

"Imagine having to wait 248 years for your next birthday!" exclaimed Ning.

"That's another point for Alaska," said Marcus.

"What else is there in the solar system?" asked Lucía, changing the subject.

"How about something that really lights up the night sky?" said Zac. He tapped his cell phone, and a ghostly image of a long strip of cloth appeared in front of them. The cloth was covered in pictures stitched in colorful thread. Most of them showed men in armor fighting.

"What's this?" asked Lucía.

"It's the Bayeux tapestry," said Zac, pronouncing it *bay YOO.* "It's a long strip of cloth with pictures sewn into it. The pictures show one of the most famous battles in history, the Battle of Hastings, in England, in 1066."

"I wanted something exciting in the night sky, not some exciting knights," joked Marcus.

"It has that, too," said Zac. "Look here at the top. See this thing that looks like a bright star with a long tail? It's a comet—Halley's Comet to be precise."

"They were doing astronomy back then?" said Marcus.

"People have been looking at the stars for as long as anyone can remember," said Zac. "But they didn't always know what they were seeing. When the comet appeared before the battle, people thought it was a bad omen for the English—a sign that the battle wouldn't go well for them."

"Was it a bad omen?" asked Ning.

"Well, it seemed that way, because the English lost," said Zac.

"So what is a comet *really?*" asked Marcus.

"A comet is a ball of ice and dust in space—like a giant, dirty snowball," said Zac. "Let's go meet the man who gave this comet its name—Sir Edmond Halley."

"Was he at the Battle of Hastings?" asked Ning.

"No," said Zac, typing into his phone. "We only need to go back as far as 1740, to Greenwich, in England."

There was a flash, and the scene changed. The space around them and the ghostly tapestry were replaced by a beautifully decorated room. By a window, there was a desk with an old-fashioned telescope on it. To the side, a man in a fancy, curled wig was taking notes. He glanced up as Zac and the others appeared.

"Ah, welcome, my young astronomers," he said. "I'm afraid you've come on a cloudy night—not good for astronomy. One cannot predict this, unfortunately."

"But you have made a prediction," said Zac.

"Yes, yes," Halley replied with a smile. "There is a comet—ah, first I should explain what a comet is..."

"It's like a bright star with a tail that appears in the sky," said Marcus.

"Yes, indeed," Halley agreed. "However, I think that comets do not appear out of nowhere. Rather, they orbit the sun on a long, stretched-out path. When they're far away, we can't see them. But as they come close, they appear in the sky. People once thought each comet was a unique event. But I think that comets return to visit us again and again at regular times."

"And you predicted when one would appear again," said Zac.

"Yes," said Halley. "I noticed that there are reports of a comet sighting about every 76 years. I predict that all these sightings are of the same comet. It should arrive again in 1758, but I'd have to live to over 100 to see it."

He peered through his window and sighed.

"This would be the same comet that appeared in 1066," said Zac.

"Yes, it is," Halley agreed. "A bad omen for King Harold, but a good one for me, I hope! It would need a name of course."

"Perhaps it should be called Halley's Comet," said Zac.

"You know, young man, I like the sound of that," said Halley with a smile.

With that, Zac tapped the screen and the scene disappeared.

Chapter 5

Star Power

After their tour of the solar system, the children felt strange being back on Earth. Orbit wandered over from the house, looking for a little attention.

"It's amazing to think that after all that, this is the only planet we can live on," said Marcus.

"Yeah, and a lot of that has to do with the sun," said Zac. "It's surprising, really—it was only a few hundred years ago that human beings realized just how important the sun is."

He quickly typed into his phone.

"I have a feeling we're about to go on another trip," said Ning. She gave Orbit a scratch behind his ears.

"You're right," said Zac. "Get ready to meet Copernicus."

FLASH!

ZUMMMMMMmmmmmmmm...

"Copernicus?" asked Lucía.

"Did someone say my name?" An old man walked slowly toward them. He had wavy gray hair. It hung down nearly to the collar of his heavy coat, which was lined with fur. "My name is Copernicus—Nicolaus Copernicus. Have you come to see my book? The printer is putting the finishing touches on it now. You will have to wait a little longer."

"No, sir, we haven't come to see the book. We came to talk to you," said Zac.

Copernicus smiled. "Then come, and we will talk. Do you mind if we sit? I'm not as healthy as I used to be." He led them to some chairs around a table.

"Where are we?" Lucía whispered to Zac. "And, what's this book he's talking about?"

"We're in Frombork, in Poland. The year is 1543. The book is called *On the Revolutions of the Celestial Spheres.*"

"That's a mouthful," said Lucía "What's it about?"

"It's about how the planets move," said Zac, "but I'll let Copernicus explain."

There was something interesting on the table. It looked like a globe made up of strips of wood, bent into hoops. In the center was a model of the sun. Orbit gave it a curious sniff. Then he curled up on the floor nearby.

"So, what is it you want to know?" asked Copernicus.

"It's about your work on the way the planets move," said Zac.

"Ah, it is very simple. We have always been told that Earth is at the center and that everything in the sky—the sun, the planets, and the stars—orbits around it."

Hearing his name, Orbit looked up eagerly.

"It makes sense. We see the sun rise, we watch it travel across the sky, and then it sinks away." Copernicus rested his hand on the model.

"However, after careful study, I think that the sun is at the center and that Earth and the other planets orbit around it." Orbit perked up again.

"So you wrote about this in your book?" said Marcus.

"Yes," Copernicus replied. "Now everyone will learn the true orbits of the planets."

Orbit was becoming confused and upset. Copernicus started coughing. The coughing fit seemed to leave him exhausted.

"We won't take any more of your time, sir," said Zac. "Thank you, and good luck with your book."

Zac hit the button on his app and the scene disappeared.

"So was the book a success?" asked Lucía.

"Well, not everyone believed Copernicus's ideas," said Zac, "but the truth was out. Unfortunately, Copernicus wouldn't see the effect of his work. He died very soon after the book was published."

"Oh, what a shame," said Lucía.

"Yes, it was," Zac agreed. "So, in honor of the great man, let's go and see the center of our solar system, the sun."

"Zac, we see the sun every day. It's that bright yellow thing in the sky," said Marcus.

"You've never seen it like this before," said Zac.

FLASH!

ZUMMMMMMmmmmmmmm...

A huge fiery ball appeared in front of them. Its whole bright surface churned, rippled, and swirled, as if it were alive. Great fiery bursts rose in loops from the surface.

"That's the sun?" breathed Lucía in wonder.

"Amazing, isn't it?" said Zac. "You wouldn't think a giant ball of gas would be so impressive."

"It's made of gas?" said Lucía.

"Yep, mainly hydrogen," Zac answered.

"So why is it on fire?" Lucía asked.

"Well, it's not actually on fire. What you are seeing is the result of a nuclear reaction," said Zac.

"What?! Like a bomb?" asked Marcus.

"Kind of. At the sun's center, hydrogen is being changed into helium," said Zac.

"How?!" said Marcus.

"Well," Zac continued, "the sun is huge. More than a million Earths would fit inside of it. It's also more than 300,000 times as heavy as Earth. The weight of all that gas pressing down creates a lot of pressure in the middle. The gas heats up so much there that it triggers nuclear fusion."

"You're losing me," said Ning.

"Everything is made up of tiny pieces called atoms. They're like the building blocks of matter. Inside the sun, atoms of the element hydrogen are being smashed together, combining them. Two atoms of hydrogen combine to make an atom of the element helium. That's called nuclear fusion," Zac explained.

"Okay, I think I get it. So is it the helium that makes the sun glow?" asked Ning.

"No," said Zac. "Along with making helium, the fusion reaction releases an incredible amount of energy. It is this energy that results in the sun's light and heat."

"And that's what we need for life on Earth…" said Marcus. "That is literally out of this world… I'm not even joking!"

"But didn't you say a while ago that the sun was a star?" asked Ning.

"Yeah, it's an average-sized star," said Zac.

"Stars get bigger than this?" said Lucía.

"Oh, yeah," said Zac. "In fact, let's talk to someone who has looked at plenty of stars. We're going back to the 1930's."

Chapter 6

Counting the Stars

Zac tapped his phone, and the sun disappeared. It was replaced by a woman sitting at a desk. She was peering through a magnifier, inspecting a plate of glass.

"That's Annie Jump Cannon," said Zac. "She developed a system that astronomers use to sort the stars into categories. She started her work in 1896. Back then, women weren't generally encouraged to have scientific careers. They weren't even allowed to vote!"

"Why is she ignoring us?" said Ning.

"She probably doesn't realize we're here. At a young age, she lost her hearing almost entirely. It may have been from a disease called scarlet fever," Zac explained. "We'd better speak up."

"Miss Cannon, I hope we're not disturbing you!" shouted Ning.

"Oh, hello. Sorry, I was at work. I'm always at work," Cannon laughed. "It's my life, really—classifying stars."

"How many stars have you classified?" asked Lucía.

"Well over 300,000, so far," Cannon replied.

"300,000!" gasped Marcus. "That must have taken forever!"

"I've been doing this for 30 years, and I've gotten quick at it," she explained. "I can classify over 200 stars an hour now. I inspect their images on these photographic plates and work it out from there."

"How do you tell them all apart?" asked Lucía.

"We know that there were different types of stars— some huge, others much smaller than the sun," Cannon explained. "The stars give out different amounts of light. I came up with a simple system that ranks them by brightness. I settled on seven different categories in the end."

"Astronomers still use that system today," added Zac. "And Annie Jump Cannon went on to classify over 350,000 stars—more than anyone in history!"

"That's amazing, Miss Cannon!" said Lucía.

"Why, thank you. If you're interested in what I do, I hope you will think about becoming a scientist, too. We could use more women in the sciences. Now, if you don't mind," she said, "I'd like to get back to my work. These stars won't classify themselves."

The friends said their goodbyes, and Zac tapped the button on the Backspace app again. The children were standing back in Zac's yard.

"I can't believe she classified that many stars," said

Lucía. "I'm starting to like the idea of space science."

"That must be all the stars in the night sky," said Marcus. He looked up at the clouds. "Too bad we can't see them now."

"Actually, you can't actually see that many, even on the clearest night," said Zac.

"How many can you see?" asked Ning.

"Around 9,000," Zac replied.

"In that case, she must have seen most of the stars that there are," said Marcus.

"Not even close," Zac answered. "Stars are arranged in groups called galaxies. Our galaxy—called the Milky Way—has between 100 billion and 400 billion stars."

"Hold on—that's a pretty big range," said Lucía.

"Well, it's hard to tell how many there are exactly," Zac explained. "We can't see them all, even with a telescope. Some are hidden by dust between us and them. Others aren't bright enough, or they are too far away. The Milky Way is huge."

"How huge?" asked Lucía.

"The nearest star to the sun is 25 trillion miles away, or 40 trillion kilometers," said Zac. "The distances between stars are so huge that we need something bigger than miles and kilometers to measure them."

"So what's that?" asked Marcus.

"Light-years," answered Zac. "One light-year is the distance light travels through space in a year."

"Light travels?" said Ning.

"Of course it does," Zac said, "but we usually don't notice because it moves so fast. Light travels 186,000 miles, or 299,000 kilometers, in a second."

"Wow, that's quick!" replied Lucía.

"And, it's a lot of miles in a year," Zac added. "5.88 trillion miles, or 9.46 trillion kilometers, to be exact. The Milky Way is about 100,000 light-years across."

"I can't wrap my brain around that," said Marcus.

"Yeah, the distance kind of blows your mind," agreed Zac. "And, to make your head hurt even more, astronomers think that there are around 100 billion other galaxies out there. Look."

Zac tapped his phone, and it projected pictures of several galaxies in front of the group of friends. "These are some of our nearest galaxies, as well as our own."

"So which one is ours?" asked Ning.

"That swirly one, there. It's a flat disk, with a bright center. These swirling arms twirl out from it. A galaxy shaped like that is called a spiral galaxy."

"What about that one?" said Lucía, pointing.

"That one's called M32, and it's an elliptical galaxy. It's shaped like a squished or stretched ball of stars."

"And what about the blobby one?" said Marcus.

"That's IC 3583. It's an irregular galaxy. Irregular galaxies don't have well-defined shapes like the others. Those are the three different kinds of galaxies."

"Why do the names get more boring?" asked Lucía. "I mean *IC-whatever* isn't as cool as *the Milky Way*."

"I know someone who can explain," said Zac.

FLASH!

ZUMMMMMMmmmmmmm...

The friends appeared in a round room with a domed metal roof. A giant telescope stretched through an opening in the dome. An older man was peering into the telescope. He wore a slightly rumpled suit and tie. He tapped an unlit pipe against his leg absent mindedly as he stared into the eyepiece.

"This is Edwin Hubble," said Zac. "He was the first person to realize that some of the faint patches of light we can see in the night sky are actually distant galaxies, as big and wonderful as our own."

"Not just that," said Hubble. He stepped away from the telescope and gave them each a handshake. "I also found that other galaxies are getting farther away from our own. Welcome to Mount Wilson Observatory. This is where I do most of my work."

"We were curious about galaxy names," said Zac.

"And why they're so boring," added Ning.

"Yes, they can be a little dull," laughed Hubble. "We astronomers keep track of things in the sky using special catalogs. For example, have you ever heard something called *M* followed by a number?"

"Like M32?" Marcus remembered.

"Exactly!" said Hubble. "The *M* stands for *Messier.* The name comes from a catalog made by the French astronomer Charles Messier, back in the late 1700's."

"What about the IC 3583?" Lucía asked.

"IC galaxies are listed in the Index Catalogue of Nebulae and Clusters of Stars," replied Hubble.

"Did you use that telescope?" asked Marcus.

"Yes, among others," replied Hubble. "It's a cold, lonely life in an observatory at night, but I love it. Here it is 1934, and I think of all the things that have been discovered. And I know one thing—we're going to keep on making new discoveries."

"We sure will," agreed Zac.

"I won't be around to see them all myself," added Hubble. "Maybe you'll be the ones to discover the next big thing. Do me proud."

Chapter 7

Probing Further

The observatory disappeared as quickly as it had flashed into existence.

"Hubble died in 1953," said Zac. "But, in a way, he's still making discoveries."

"What do you mean?" asked Lucía.

"There's a telescope that was named in his honor—but not just an ordinary telescope. This telescope was launched into space in 1990. It orbits Earth, where it can take pictures of the universe without the atmosphere getting in the way."

"Amazing!" said Ning. "I bet that would have made Edwin Hubble really happy."

"I'm sure it would. Of course, the Hubble Space Telescope is just one of the machines we've sent into space to discover more about the universe," said Zac.

"We've sent other things out there?" asked Marcus.

"We've sent tons of probes," said Zac. "A probe is a spacecraft that collects information about what's around it. There are no astronauts on a probe, so it can keep flying around for years and years."

"What kind of things do probes look for?" asked Lucía.

"All kinds of stuff," said Zac. "Some visit the various planets and other objects in our solar system. Others orbit the planets or actually land on them to tell us what conditions are like on the surface."

"Can we go and see one?" said Ning.

"It's no problem for the Backspace app," said Zac with a smile.

FLASH!

ZUMMMMMMmmmmmmm...

"Hey, I recognize this place," said Marcus. "This is Mars again."

"Correct," said Zac. "And here comes what I wanted you to see."

A strange-looking vehicle with six wheels rolled slowly toward them over the dusty Martian plain.

"Is that a car? I thought you said that astronauts had not yet landed on Mars!" said Lucía.

"Or is it some kind of weird Martian?" said Marcus.

Zac laughed. "No, there are no astronauts and no Martians. This is Curiosity. It's a type of probe called a rover. Think of it as an oversized remote control car—something between that and a rolling robot."

The rover rolled up to the friends and came to a halt. It was the size of a small car, but it had no doors or windows. Instead, it had lots of parts and odd instruments sticking out all over it.

"So, who's driving this thing?" asked Marcus walking around the rover.

"Scientists back on Earth send it instructions about where to go."

"What does it do?" asked Ning.

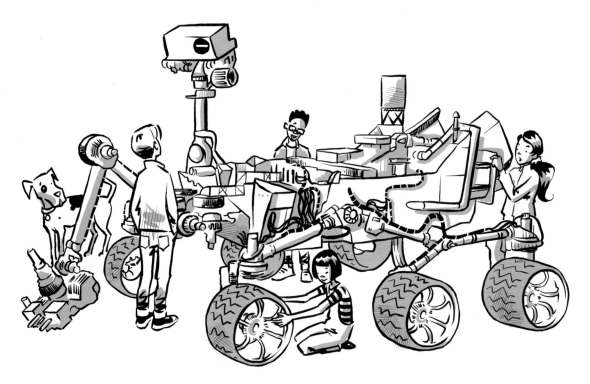

"What doesn't it do, more like it," Zac replied. "For starters, it has cameras to send back pictures. It has these devices called spectrometers that can tell us all kinds of things, such as what kinds of minerals are in the rocks."

"Is that the camera?" said Marcus, leaning towards one of the instruments. He gave a cheesy grin and waved. "If this was real, that would really freak out those scientists back on Earth."

They all laughed.

"The funny thing is, we're kind of hoping for something like that," said Zac. "Let me show you."

He tapped the screen of his cell phone, and the dusty surface of Mars was replaced with the bright light of a large, clean laboratory. In the center of the room was a large spacecraft. The top part of the craft was a big satellite dish. People wearing white coveralls and dust masks were inspecting the craft and making adjustments.

"It's 1977," said Zac. "That's one of the two Voyager probes. It's being prepared for launch."

"So what's it going to do?" asked Lucía.

"The Voyager probes were built to visit Jupiter, Saturn, Uranus, and Neptune, which they did. They beamed back tons of information, but that's not why we're here. I wanted to you to see that," Zac said, pointing.

The children watched workers attach a golden circle to the side of the probe.

"Inside that cover is a golden record—a little gold disk with grooves on it. Each of the Voyagers carried one. The grooves on the record hold all kinds of information about Earth, including recordings of different sounds: people

talking, whale song, different kinds of music, stuff like that."

"Why?" asked Lucía.

"In case any aliens ever find it," said Zac. "They might be able to figure out how to play the record and learn about Earth."

"But we've seen the planets the probes visited," said Lucía. "There's no life there."

"Yes, but people weren't sure of that in 1977. Besides, the mission planners knew that after the Voyagers whizzed past the outer planets, they would sail off into space. In the early 2000's, both Voyagers reached the edge of the solar system and showed no sign of stopping."

"Where are they going?" asked Ning.

"Just out into space," said Zac. "Scientists hope that the batteries will last a few more years, so the probes can continue to send back information. But even when we lose contact, the Voyagers will just keep on flying."

"So there's hope that someone, somewhere, will find a golden record someday," said Marcus.

"It's a pretty slight chance, but yeah, that's the idea."

"So is there life out there?" asked Ning.

"Now that," said Zac reaching for his phone to turn off the app, "is a pretty big question."

Chapter 8

Goldilocks

Back in the front yard, Zac dug around in his pocket and pulled out a handful of junk. There was some string, a magnet, and a few crumpled pieces of paper.

"Ah, here it is," he said, finding a piece of chalk. He crouched to draw on the pavement of the driveway.

"This big circle is the sun," he said, "and these are the planets in our solar system. I haven't spaced them out to scale, because the driveway isn't nearly long enough."

"What's with all the graffiti?" asked Ning.

"Aliens!" said Zac. "Or, to be precise, our hunt for aliens."

"But we know there are no aliens in the solar system. You said so," said Lucía.

"As far as we know, but..." Zac drew a line on either side of his drawing of Earth, "...we do know that planets within a certain distance from their star can have the right conditions for life. In particular, they can have liquid water on their surface."

"Okay…" said Marcus.

"Wherever we find life on Earth, it depends on liquid water," Zac continued. "So, looking for water seems like a good way to start looking for life. Venus is much too hot for liquid water. Mars is too cold, at least on the surface. But Earth is at the right distance from the sun for liquid water. Scientists call this region the 'habitable zone.' It's also called the 'Goldilocks zone,' like in the folk tale."

"Because it's not too hot and not too cold, like the baby bear's porridge!" said Lucía.

"Exactly. So scientists are looking for these Goldilocks planets, as they be home to life."

"But how do they find these planets?" asked Ning.

"And how will we see

them? The nearest stars are trillions of miles away, and planets are smaller than stars," Lucía protested.

"Remember the Hubble telescope?" Zac asked. "They're using another space telescope. This one is called Kepler. It's named after a German astronomer from the 1600's."

"They can see the planets using Kepler?" said Marcus.

"Not really," said Zac, "The planets are too dim and too close to their stars to be seen directly. What Kepler does is scan thousands of stars, monitoring their brightness. Occasionally, a star will dim ever so slightly. The dimming is caused by a planet passing in front of its star, blocking some of the light."

"Like an eclipse?" asked Marcus.

"Kind of," said Zac.

"So, has Kepler found any Goldilocks planets?" asked Lucía.

"It has!" said Zac, excited. "So far, it's discovered several planets that are about the size of Earth and that are probably rocky, like Earth is. Some may orbit in their star's Goldilocks zone."

"So, do they have any life on them?" asked Marcus.

"Well, the first question is do they have any water," said Zac.

"Do they have any water?" Marcus mocked.

"We don't know. Kepler can't tell us that," Zac admitted.

"That's kind of disappointing," said Marcus.

"But, scientists are always building bigger telescopes," said Zac. "One day, they may be able to detect traces of water on distant planets, or even life."

"How big can a telescope be?" said Ning.

"Way bigger than this thing," said Zac, patting his own telescope. "The mirror in my telescope is only 70 millimeters across, or about 2 3/4 inches. There are telescopes with mirrors dozens of feet or meters across. But even that's tiny compared to some radio telescopes."

"I didn't know there were different kinds of telescopes," said Lucía.

"Oh, yeah," said Zac. "In fact, if you want to see a big telescope, I know just the place!"

FLASH!

ZUMMMMmmmmmmm...

"Wow, where are we?" asked Lucía. The friends stood in the middle of a vast gray bowl. Stretching above them was a huge triangle of metal poles, with what looked like a gigantic golf ball hanging from it. It was held in place by thick metal wires attached to giant supports.

"I feel like a corn flake in a cereal bowl," said Ning.

"We're in Puerto Rico," said Zac, "and this is the Arecibo Observatory radio telescope."

"What do you mean *radio* telescope?" asked Lucía. "Does this thing play music?"

"Telescopes like mine look for visible light coming from space," Zac explained. "They're called optical telescopes. But there are other kinds of light we can't see, like radio waves. Radio telescopes detect and study these invisible waves. No music—sorry."

"It's absolutely huge," said Ning.

"It is," agreed Zac. "It's 1,000 feet, or 300 meters, across. Think of it like a giant mirror for gathering radio waves."

"So why did you bring us here, Zac?" said Marcus.

"I brought you here because we were talking about life on other planets," said Zac. "This telescope has been used to listen for signs of alien life."

"What kind of signs?" said Lucía.

"Like voices?" said Marcus.

"It's hard to imagine what an alien signal might be like," said Zac. "Aliens might be very different from us. Scientists hope that any aliens would send some kind of regular signal, an organized one that couldn't be confused with anything natural."

"Has this telescope found anything?" said Ning.

"It's detected some strange signals before, but no definite proof that they were sent by aliens," said Zac.

"But that means that aliens could be out there," said Marcus excitedly.

"It's too bad we can't just call them first," said Lucía.

"Well, we've tried, actually," said Zac. "In 1974,

this telescope sent a radio signal to a small bunch of stars."

"Have we gotten an answer yet?" asked Marcus, even more excited than before.

"No, and don't hold your breath," Zac answered. "Remember that distances in space are huge, even when you travel as fast as light. It'll take around 25,000 years for the message to even reach the star cluster."

"We'll never find anything living in space at this rate!" huffed Marcus.

"But look at it this way—if we can send messages to the stars, we can send them to your new house in Alaska," said Zac.

"Yeah, of course—we can video chat and text and stuff," said Ning.

"Yeah, I suppose," said Marcus, but he still sounded disappointed.

Chapter 9

Is There Anybody Out There?

The Arecibo Observatory disappeared from sight, and the friends found themselves back in Zac's yard. Lucía looked up at the night sky.

"You know, I think the clouds are beginning to break up a bit," she said. "We might actually get some use from your telescope after all."

"I think you might be right," said Zac, unpacking the equipment he had begun to put away earlier. Orbit wandered over to see if there was anything interesting in the box. "You seem to have developed a new interest in space," Zac said to Lucía.

"I never realized that there was so much interesting stuff up there," she answered.

"No chance of finding anything living up there, though," said Marcus.

"You know, that's not strictly true. If it was clear, I could show you somewhere people can and do live in space," said Zac.

"Can't you just take us there with the Backspace app?" said Marcus.

FLASH!

ZUMMMMMMmmmmmmm...

The friends were in the strangest room they had ever visited. To begin with, the walls weren't completely square. Looking from the side, they could see the room was six-sided in shape, more like a hexagon. Every surface was covered in screens, keyboards, wires, blinking lights, and other equipment. The place was also very brightly lit.

"I'm floating!" shrieked Lucía.

"You're virtually floating," corrected Zac.

"Well, in that case, I'm virtually loving it," said Ning with a huge smile on her face. She turned a quick somersault. "This is great! I'm not sure Orbit likes it, though."

Orbit looked a little confused as he drifted by, pawing helplessly at the air.

"How does this work, Zac?" asked Marcus.

"The app has tricked your mind into thinking you're floating in microgravity—the weightlessness felt by astronauts in orbit. If you stamped your feet hard enough, you'd feel the driveway underneath you," Zac explained.

"Where are we?" asked Lucía, once she had gotten used to the feeling of virtual weightlessness.

"This is the International Space Station," said Zac. "It's a huge spacecraft—it's almost the size of a football field. It's in orbit—sorry, Orbit—around Earth, 220 miles or 350 kilometers above the planet's surface. Astronauts have lived here since 2000."

"So where are they?" asked Marcus.

"Right here," said a voice.

The friends turned around as a woman floated toward them. She wore a blue jumpsuit, and her hair was pulled back in a ponytail.

"Welcome to the International Space Station."

"You work here?" asked Lucía.

"Yes, I'm one of the astronauts on board," she answered. "There are three of us. Right now, we're studying how life in space affects the human body."

"Is that what the astronauts here always do?" asked Marcus.

"We do all kinds of different experiments here. But even just spending time here is an experiment, in a way. As you've probably noticed, life on the space station is very different from life on Earth."

"Yeah, I'm not sure I could get used to all this floating," said Marcus.

"And, you have to remember that everything floats. If you spill a drink, it floats—look."

The astronaut took a water bottle and emptied a bit into the air. Instead of falling, the water split into wobbly droplets that floated in the air.

"Try catching them in your mouth!" she suggested, nudging Lucía.

Lucía floated toward the droplets with her mouth open, tilting her head to catch every last one. She giggled as she swallowed the cool water.

"That's so much fun!" said Lucía.

"It's great, isn't it? I never get bored of it," said the astronaut. "Sleeping is a little weird, though. You have to strap yourself into bed so you don't float away."

She pointed to a sleeping bag strapped to the wall.

"But how can you sleep hanging from the wall?" asked Ning.

"It doesn't matter which way is up, here," said the astronaut.

"Where is everybody?" asked Zac, looking around.

"Well, the other two astronauts are out there."

She pointed out one of the windows. Two astronauts were floating outside in space suits, working on the space station's outer surface.

"What are they doing?" asked Marcus.

"Just a little routine maintenance," she answered.

"That looks amazing!" said Ning.

"It is," the astronaut agreed. "I've only been out once so far, but I can't wait to do it again. I love it here on the station—It's like a laboratory with the best view ever."

The friends looked out of the window to see Earth. The planet was loosely wrapped in white clouds. The bright blue of the oceans beneath showed through.

"What I like about seeing Earth from here is that you see continents, not countries," the astronaut explained. "The planet looks united, just like it is up here, with people from across the world working together."

"I can still see Alaska," announced Marcus.

"I'd love to work here," said Lucía. "But traveling in a cramped rocket would freak me out."

"Oh, don't let the journey stop you from reaching your destination," the astronaut said. "Taking off in rockets to get here totally freaks me out. But then I think about where I'm going and why. Suddenly, doesn't feel so bad."

"I suppose so," said Lucía.

"And it was much worse for the first astronauts," said Zac.

"Was it ever!" said the astronaut. "I think about my heroes, like Sally Ride—she was an astronaut and a physicist, like me. Space travel was a lot more terrifying back then, because we didn't know as much about it as we do now."

"And the technology wasn't yet developed," added Zac.

"No," she agreed. "We owe the first astronauts a great deal of gratitude for their bravery. And we owe animals like your dog there our gratitude, too."

"Oh, I was trying to hide Orbit," said Ning. "I didn't think he'd be allowed up here."

The scientist laughed. "Dogs were in space before people! In fact, lots of animals were. The first animal to go into orbit was a Russian dog named Laika. That was back in 1957. It was another seven years before humans made it."

"Which is why you're called Orbit, Orbit," said Zac

patting his dog's head.

"Now, I'm sorry to say I have some work to do," the astronaut explained, "so I'll say goodbye. Maybe I'll get to work with you in the future."

"Yes, I'd like that," said Lucía.

They waved goodbye to the astronaut. Zac tapped the screen of his phone, and the scene disappeared.

Chapter 10

Cosmic Questions

After visiting the International Space Station, Zac's front yard didn't seem very exciting. Lucía looked at the cloudy sky with longing.

"We must know a lot about space now," she said. "I wonder if there will even be anything left to discover by the time I'm old enough to go into space for real."

"Oh, there'll be plenty left," said Zac.

"What kinds of things?" said Ning.

"There are plenty of mysteries left in space," Zac replied. "Take black holes, for example."

"Black holes? What are they?" asked Ning.

"Well, black holes are what can happen when a large star dies. All that matter has such a strong gravitational pull that it collapses in on itself. As it gets smaller and denser, its gravitational pull gets stronger and stronger. It becomes so strong that nothing can escape it," said Zac.

"Nothing?"

"Nothing—not even light." Zac answered. "That's why they're called black holes. And the more stuff they suck in, the stronger their pull becomes."

"That sounds like a drain in space," said Lucía.

"Sounds like Alaska to me, sucking me in where I'll disappear from view," said Marcus.

"Don't be silly—you know we'll visit," said Lucía.

"How many black holes are there?" asked Ning.

"No one knows," said Zac, "but scientists think there's a huge one in the middle of our galaxy."

"No way!" said Marcus.

"Don't worry, we're far enough away that it won't get us," said Zac.

"Still, that's freaking me out! Are there any space

mysteries that aren't going to mess with my head?" asked Ning.

"Well, there's dark matter," said Zac. "Astronomers can figure out the mass of all the stars and other things that we can see. But when they watch it all in motion, there's something missing. There's not enough mass for gravity to hold it all together. They know there must be even more mass than what we can see."

"What does that mean?" asked Lucía.

"It means there's something there that we can't see," Zac explained. "So they called it 'dark' matter."

"Whoa, that's freaky," said Ning.

"Maybe they just can't see dark matter because the rest of space is so dark," said Marcus.

"It's a good thought, but even in space, objects are either shining out light, reflecting it, or blocking it. Dark matter doesn't do any of these things. That's a mystery that I'd like to solve," said Zac.

"Not only that," he continued. "But there's dark energy, too. It's a mysterious kind of energy that's pushing the galaxies from one another, faster and faster. Nobody knows what it is."

Just when it looked like Zac would go on forever, Marcus's cell phone rang. He wandered down the driveway to answer the call in private. Seconds later, he was back, smiling.

"That was my mom," he said. "She's just heard that there's another job open where she works now. We're not going to Alaska, after all!"

The friends high-fived joyously.

"I guess parts of it would have been cool—cold, even," Marcus admitted. "But I'm glad I don't have to move away from you all. Catch you all later!"

As Marcus left, Zac saw that the clouds had cleared.

"Hey, we can use this telescope after all!" Zac said. "And look, quick! That light going across the sky, that's the International Space Station!"

The friends watched the tiny dot trace a path across the heavens.

"In a way, it's too bad Marcus isn't moving," said Zac. "I was looking forward to a real trip to Alaska. I'm ready for a break from all this virtual travel."

"Not me, I like having Marcus around—just don't tell him that," said Ning.

"I like having him around, too," said Lucía as she watched the International Space Station disappear out of sight. "And as for travel, if everything goes according to plan, one day I'll be going somewhere much farther away than Alaska."

Meet the Scientists

Neil Armstrong

Neil Armstrong (1930-2012) was an American engineer, test pilot, and astronaut. In 1969, he became the first person to walk on the surface of the moon.

Johann Bode

Johann Bode (*YOH hahn BOW duh*) (1747-1826) was a German astronomer. He is most famous for describing the orbit of Uranus and suggesting the planet's name. He was left practically blind in his right eye following a childhood illness.

Edmond Halley

Edmond Halley (*HAL ee*) (1656-1742) was a British mathematician and astronomer. He correctly predicted the return of the comet that now bears his name.

Nicolaus Copernicus

Nicolaus Copernicus *(nihk uh LAY uhs koh PUR nuh kuhs)* (1473-1543) was a Polish mathematician and astronomer. His argument that the planets orbit the sun caused uproar across Europe.

Annie Jump Cannon

Annie Jump Cannon (1863-1941) was an American astronomer. Her greatest achievement was to develop a system of classifying different types of stars. A variation of her system is still used today.

Edwin Hubble

Edwin Hubble (1889-1953) was an American astronomer. Hubble determined that some of the things we can see in space are actually distant galaxies. He also proved that the universe is *expanding* (getting bigger).

Glossary

astronomy the study of objects in the heavens

atmosphere the gases that surround a planet

atmospheric pressure the weight of the overlying air pressing down all around

crater a hole made by the impact of a meteorite or comet

dwarf planet a round object somewhat smaller than a planet that orbits a star

elliptical galaxy a galaxy that is a stretched circle shape

friction the resistance between two objects that rub against each other

galaxy a large group of stars

gas giant a large planet made mostly of gas

gravity the force of attraction between objects with mass. On the surface of Earth or any other massive body, gravity pulls things downward.

irregular galaxy a galaxy with no obvious structure

nuclear fusion the combining of two smaller atoms to make a bigger one, releasing energy. The fusion of hydrogen to helium produces the energy given off by the sun and other stars.

observatory a building with a telescope in it for looking at the stars

optical telescope a telescope for viewing visible light from the stars

probe an unmanned space vehicle

selfie an informal self-portrait, usually taken with a cell phone

spiral galaxy a galaxy with arms that spin out from a central bulge

virtual created and existing only in a computer—like the historical scenes visited in Zac's Backspace app

Additional Resources

Books

Professor Astro Cat's Frontiers of Space, Ben Newman
(Flying Eye Books, 2013)

The Solar System, Meteors and Comets, Clive Gifford
(Wayland, 2016)

Space: A Children's Encyclopedia
(DK Children, 2010)

Space Encyclopedia: A Tour of Our Solar System and Beyond, David
Aguilar (National Geographic Kids, 2013)

Websites

ESA Kids
https://www.esa.int/esaKIDSen/

General information on space and space exploration from the European
Space Agency.

Solar System Exploration
https://solarsystem.nasa.gov/kids/index.cfm

Information, activities, and games about the solar system from the home
of American space exploration, NASA.

Universe Facts
https://www.natgeokids.com/uk/discover/science/space/universe-facts/

A range of information and facts from National Geographic.

Index